THE
WEALTH
RIPPLE

Break the Cycle. Build Financial Freedom.
Transform Your Family's Future

CASSANDRA M. THOMAS

Cassandra M. Thomas-- 1ˢᵗ ed.
Chief Editor, Shannon Buritz
ISBN: 978-1-954757-57-8

The information provided in this book is for educational and informational purposes only and is not intended as financial, legal, tax, or investment advice. While every effort has been made to ensure the accuracy and effectiveness of the content, the author and publisher make no guarantees regarding the outcomes of applying the strategies discussed.

Readers are encouraged to consult with a qualified financial advisor, tax professional, or legal expert before making any financial decisions. The author and publisher expressly disclaim any liability for any loss or risk, personal or otherwise, incurred as a consequence of the use and application of any of the information contained in this book.

Financial education is a personal journey, and results may vary based on individual circumstances, choices, and efforts. This book does not promise or guarantee specific financial results. The goal is to empower readers to take informed steps toward financial wellness and long-term wealth.

While all attempts have been made to verify information provided in this publication, the publisher assumes no responsibility for errors, omissions, or contrary interpretation of the subject matter herein. Any perceived slights of specific persons, peoples, or organizations are unintentional.

To my beloved family—my husband, Damon, and my daughters, Damonique and Taymana —thank you for your unwavering love, strength, and encouragement.

To my precious grandchildren—Jerramani, Jerra'Myah, Cassidy, and Jamari—this book is especially dedicated to you. You represent the first of many generations who will rise with the financial knowledge, head start, and confidence to build lives of purpose, abundance, and legacy. May you always walk boldly toward the future with wisdom and wealth at your side.

And to every head of household who is struggling financially or silently wondering if there's more, you are right. This is for those who dream of a better life, who long to make better financial choices, and who are determined to shift the trajectory for themselves and those they love. You are not alone. You are capable. And your journey to more begins now.

CONTENTS

INTRODUCTION

Imagine waking up every day without the nagging worry of whether you have enough money—enough for today, the future, enough to live the life you truly want. No more sleepless nights over rent, mortgage payments, or bills. No more scrambling to make ends meet. Instead, you have the peace of mind from knowing you're making smart financial decisions today that will set you up for a better tomorrow. That's the kind of freedom I want for you.

It's not just about your financial well-being—it's also about how your financial literacy can impact the people around you. Whether it's your kids, siblings, or close friends, someone in our lives always finds themselves in a money bind. Wouldn't it be nice to help them when they need it and be the one to guide them toward better money management so they don't keep falling into the same traps? When you take control of your finances, you become a beacon of hope, showing those around you how to make informed choices that build a secure future.

I'll never forget the excitement of getting my first credit card in college. If you've ever been on a college campus, you know how it goes—credit card companies show up, offering what seems like the best deal ever. "Here, take this card! You're approved!" And at that age, without much knowledge, it feels like free money. I was young and in school, and I wasn't thinking long-term. I remember buying this beautiful black long coat—it was on sale, and I *love* a good sale. I was so excited, feeling like I had made a smart purchase. I had a job, but I wasn't making much, and my focus was on my education, not managing money.

That coat may have been on sale at the store, but I ended up paying *three times* its price because I didn't fully understand how credit worked. Late payments and interest charges made that "great deal" a huge burden. That coat became my first lesson in how financial decisions can have long-term consequences, especially when you don't have the proper knowledge.

Looking back, I wish someone had told me the truth about credit before I got that first card. I wish I had understood the responsibility that came with it. But that's exactly why I'm writing this book—because I don't want you to learn these lessons the hard way like I did.

We spend years in school learning math, science, and history. But when it comes to managing money, we're left with barely a lesson or two, maybe a couple of word problems in math class.

No one sits down with us and says, "Here's how you budget, how you save, how you make smart choices that will set you up for the future." Due to this lack of education, our country is currently in a financial literacy epidemic. If our parents didn't know how to manage money, they couldn't teach us either. So we enter adulthood without the financial foundation we need, and by the time we realize it, we're already playing catch-up.

And then there is the dreaded "B" word: budgeting. People hear that word and immediately shut down. Some think they don't need it—"I know where my money is going, I don't need to track it." Others think it's too complicated—"I can't sit down and give every single dollar a job." But without a budget, you're flying blind, just hoping you'll have enough left over at the end of the month. A budget actually gives you control. It's the key to covering your current expenses and saving for retirement or those big goals you dream about but never feel like you can afford. Without it, financial stability will always feel just out of reach.

I see this struggle firsthand, even in my own family. My daughter is on this journey right now, and it's a process. I keep telling her, "You need a budget, you need a budget," but she pushes back. "What's the point of a budget if I barely have enough to cover what I need?" she says.

And that's the mindset so many people have—the idea that budgeting is only for people who already have extra money. But that's exactly *why* you need one! Without it, money disappears before you even realize where it went.

For a lot of people, the biggest fear about money is simply *not having enough*. The anxiety of being broke, of never making enough to get ahead, is paralyzing. It's that thought of, *Why even try if I'm always going to be in the negative?* This fear keeps people from addressing their finances because they feel that no effort will make a difference.

Another huge barrier is not knowing where to start. Money management feels overwhelming, and when something feels unfamiliar, it's easy to avoid it altogether. People worry about doing it wrong—what's the *right* way to budget? What if they make mistakes? The truth is that there's no one-size-fits-all budget. There's no magic formula that works for everyone. The plan has to fit *your* situation and help you make small, intentional changes to move in a better direction.

One of the biggest myths I hear is that being on a budget means you can't enjoy life. People think budgeting means counting every single dollar and never doing anything fun. But a budget doesn't mean *you can't go out to eat or enjoy yourself*—it means you plan for it. You give every dollar a job, including the money you set aside for fun. The difference is that now you're spending with intention instead of wondering where all your money went at the end of the month.

Let's clear up some of the biggest money myths right now:

1. **"Money is the root of all evil."**

   No, it's not. The *love* of money at the expense of every-thing else might lead people down the wrong path, but money itself? It's a tool. It can be used for good. It can provide stability and opportunities and even allow you to help others.

2. **"Only the rich can afford to invest."**

   Completely false. Investing isn't just for millionaires—anyone wanting to build a stronger financial future. The real risk is not investing at all and missing out on the opportunity to grow your money over time.

3. **"All debt is bad."**

   Not true. There's a vast difference between good debt and bad debt. A mortgage? A student loan? These can be investments in your future. But using a credit card to buy the latest iPhone or designer bag? That's bad debt—it drains your resources without giving you any-thing in return.

4. **"If I'm on a budget, I can't have fun."**

   Again, wrong! A budget doesn't mean restriction—it means control. It allows you to enjoy life while making sure your financial priorities are covered first.

5. **"People with big houses and fancy cars don't have money problems."**
   Just because someone *looks* wealthy doesn't mean they are. Many people with high incomes still struggle with money because they don't manage it well. Money issues aren't just for people who are struggling—they can affect anyone at any income level.

Not to mention, even the people with big houses and fancy cars might *not* be living the life they portray. We live in a world dominated by social media influencers. Scroll through TikTok, YouTube, or Instagram, and what do you see? People living their *best* lives—vacationing on islands, sipping mojitos, dressed in designer clothes, dining in the finest restaurants. And if you're watching from the outside, it's easy to start thinking, *This is what success looks like. This is what I should be striving for.*

But many of these influencers rent luxury cars, pose in homes they don't own, and take trips sponsored by brands. What you're seeing is a curated highlight reel—not reality. That lifestyle *costs* money. And if you're trying to keep up with it—spending on trips, expensive outings, and things you can't really afford—you're setting yourself up for financial disaster. Trying to "keep up with the Joneses" is a fast track to being broke.

And I know it's not just social media that pressures you to spend—it can also be the people closest to you. Maybe you have friends or family members who live only for today, spending without a care for the future. If you decide to take a different path—to save, to budget, to be mindful of your money, you might hear things like: *"Oh, come on, don't be so boring!" "You're really going to stay home instead of coming out with us?"*

That kind of peer pressure can make you second-guess your choices. But please remember you are not responsible for anyone else's financial habits. Your job is to make decisions that set *you* and your family up for a secure future. The people who tease you now won't be the ones paying your bills later.

One more type of negative pressure hits a nerve for me because I see it happening all the time: entire industries that *prey* on people who don't know any better. Look at lower-income neighborhoods, and what do you find on every corner? Pawn shops, title loan companies, and check cashing facilities.

These businesses are not there to help people. They exist to keep people in a cycle of debt. They target those who don't have other options, offering quick cash but charging outrageous fees and interest rates that make it nearly impossible to get ahead. They *look* like they're on your side, but their entire purpose is to keep you dependent on them. If you're already struggling financially, the last thing you need is to be giving more of your hard-earned money to businesses designed to take advantage of you. Understanding these traps is the first step to avoiding them.

You don't have to be a victim of these enemies— social media pressures, friends and family, or predatory businesses. The power to change your financial future is in *your* hands. The key is awareness. When you recognize the traps, you can make better choices. And that's what this book is all about—helping you see the obstacles holding you back and giving you the tools to move forward. No matter where you are today, financial freedom is possible. But it starts with making *intentional* choices that serve *you.*

In the following pages, I'll answer some of the most pressing questions people have about managing money effectively:

- *"What is the best way to budget my income?"*
- *"How much should I save for emergencies?"*
- *"Should I be contributing to my retirement even if I'm struggling?"*
- *"How can I reduce my daily expenses without feeling deprived?"*
- *"How do I set realistic financial goals?"*
- *"How do I improve my money management skills?"*

I've been where you are. I've made bad money decisions. I've mismanaged money, learned the hard way, and paid the price—literally. One of my biggest mistakes? I withdrew a significant amount from my 401(k) without fully understanding the consequences and ended up with a hefty tax penalty. That was a painful lesson, but it shaped the way I think about money today.

Because I've been through financial struggles myself, I know exactly how overwhelming it feels. I understand the frustration of feeling like you can't get ahead, the regret of making mistakes, and the fear of not knowing where to begin. But I also know it's possible to turn things around. Through trial and error, I learned how to make smarter choices—and now, I'm passionate about helping others do the same. I'm here to help you understand money in a clear and practical way. I've earned several credit and financial education certifications. Beyond these credentials, my real expertise comes from lived experience—both my own and working with people actively changing their financial lives.

One example that stands out is a young man I worked with in 2024. He was getting married in 2025, and when we started, he didn't have a financial plan in place. However, as a result of our working sessions together, he saved $10,000 toward his wedding and saw a *huge* boost in his credit score. That's just one story, but I've seen time and time again that small, intentional steps lead to big changes. You don't have to start with thousands of dollars. You can start an investment account with as little as $5. You can build an emergency fund one paycheck at a time. And when you gain that control, you don't just change your life—you create a ripple effect. Your kids, your family, and your friends will see the difference. You'll become the person who breaks the cycle of struggle and sets the foundation for generational wealth.

The first step is simply deciding that you want something better. You don't have to be perfect. You don't have to have it all figured out. You just need to make the decision to change, create a realistic plan, and commit to taking action, one step at a time.

Years ago, I dreamed of opening a financial education center—somewhere people could come and learn how to manage money, avoid traps, and build a better financial future. I envisioned being in a specific downtown storefront location. I even ordered little financial education booklets to get started. But life happened, and I never got the chance to bring that vision to life.

Until now.

This book *is* that financial education center. It's my way of reaching and helping as many people as possible, giving them the basic financial tools they need to change their lives. And not just their lives but the lives of their children, their families, and generations to come. It's time to let go of the stress and start making real progress. No more living paycheck to paycheck. No more feeling trapped by debt. No more believing that success is for "other people."

Financial freedom is for you, too. Let's begin.

- Cassandra M. Thomas

PART ONE
UNDERSTANDING YOUR FINANCIAL REALITY

CHAPTER ONE

Why Financial Literacy Matters
(And How It Impacts Every Part of Your Life)

Financial literacy is the difference between having a smart, productive relationship with money versus a bad, unproductive one. Without a plan for your money, you won't get ahead. Think about it—how will you pay your bills on time if you don't have a plan? And paying your bills on time matters because it directly impacts your credit score. What about saving for emergencies? Without savings, every unexpected expense could throw you into debt. And what about those opportunities that come your way—investments, career moves, or homeownership? If you're not financially literate, you won't be in a position to take advantage of them.

One of the most important things financial literacy does is help you prepare for retirement. None of us want to work forever. You want the financial freedom to enjoy your later years without worrying about money.

Financial literacy helps you make good decisions and, just as importantly, helps you to avoid the bad ones. A single financial mistake can lead to bankruptcy, debt that's hard to escape, or even the loss of things you've worked hard for. And when that happens, you're not just dealing with the consequences today— you're dealing with them for years down the line.

The goal is simple: Save money, don't squander it. Build wealth for the future, not just for the moment. Because when you know how to manage your money wisely, you create security, stability, and opportunity for yourself and the generations that follow.

Financial Literacy is for Everyone, No Matter How Much You Make

Financial literacy is required regardless of where you fall on the income scale—whether you're living paycheck to paycheck or making six or seven figures—because financial mistakes don't discriminate.

If you're in a lower income bracket, one wrong decision—like taking out a payday loan—can send you into a never-ending cycle of debt. The fees are so high that you're constantly playing catch-up, borrowing more to cover what you owe. It's a bottomless pit; without the right knowledge, it's incredibly hard to climb out.

If you're middle class, financial pitfalls look different but can be just as damaging. You may make a bad investment—stocks, bonds, or even a business venture with a friend you didn't properly vet. One slight misstep here could result in losing thousands of dollars.

And even if you're making a high income, that doesn't mean you're financially secure. In fact, plenty of high earners are drowning in debt because they're living way beyond their means.

When you're making a lot of money, it's easy to fall into the trap of spending even more—bigger houses, fancier cars, extravagant vacations. But if your spending is outpacing your income, you're setting yourself up for disaster.

That's why financial literacy matters for *everyone*. If you don't know how to manage your money wisely, it won't matter how big your paycheck is.

Why You Can't Afford to Wait

When someone lacks financial knowledge, they're usually not making smart money choices. They aren't budgeting or planning for the future, and they're stuck in a pattern such as living paycheck to paycheck—never getting ahead.

One of the biggest mistakes people make is waiting too long to start investing. The sooner you invest, the better off you'll be. Time is one of the most powerful factors in building wealth. The longer your money has to grow, the more you benefit from compounding—what Albert Einstein called the "eighth wonder of the world."

Let's break it down with an example:

- If you start investing **$500 a month** at **age 24** and earn an average return of 7%, by the time you reach **65**, your investments could grow to **$1.5 million.**
- If you **wait until 30** to start? That number drops to **$920,000.**
- If you put it off until **40**, you're looking at just **$380,000.**
- And if you wait until **50**, you'll only have **$160,000.**

That's a huge difference. Every year you wait is money lost. The best time to start managing your finances was yesterday. The second-best time is right now.

The Link Between Money, Mental Health, and Relationships

If you've ever felt the stress of not knowing how you're going to pay your rent or electricity bill or just make it through the month, you know how much financial struggles impact every part of your life. When money is tight, there's this constant feeling of uneasiness—this worrisome weight that never quite lifts.

When financial pressure builds up, your brain goes into fight, flight, or freeze mode. This is a natural response, but when it comes to money, it often leads to rash decisions and impulsive behaviors. Maybe you grab a payday loan to cover a bill, even though you know the interest is outrageous. Perhaps you put something on a credit card because it feels like the only option. Or maybe you just freeze—ignoring your situation altogether because it feels too overwhelming to deal with.

And the cycle continues. **Bad financial habits create stress, and stress leads to more bad financial decisions.**

Here's something important to note: Seven out of ten adults live in a state of chronic stress, resulting in:

- **Loss of sleep:** Tossing and turning at night, worrying about how to make ends meet.

- **Lack of motivation:** Feeling stuck, like you'll never get ahead no matter what you do.
- **Anxiety and depression**: The constant pressure of financial struggles can take a serious toll on mental health.
- **Inability to focus:** Stress clouds judgment, making it even harder to think clearly about money.

When someone is constantly stressed about money, it seeps into every interaction. It can make them short-tempered, distracted, or emotionally unavailable. They may not be present for their spouse, family, or even their job because they're overwhelmed by worry.

And then there's the shame and regret that people don't always discuss. Instead, they withdraw. They might avoid conversations with their spouse or stop engaging with friends and family. In fact, according to Forbes, 20% to 40% of marriages end due to financial issues.

The good news is you don't have to live like this. The more you understand your money, the less stress you carry. Learning to budget, plan, and make smart decisions doesn't just improve your bank account—it improves your mental health and, in turn, your relationships.

A Shift in Perspective

Sometimes, all it takes is one shift in perspective to change your financial future completely. I know this from personal experience. For years, my husband and I had a habit of getting close to paying off a car, and then what did we do? We'd trade it in for a newer model. And to keep the payments low, we'd take out the longest-term loan possible. It seemed like a wise move at the time: lower payments, a newer car.

But here's what we didn't realize: Stretching out those payments meant we paid way more in interest. Instead of working toward true financial freedom, we were trapped in a never-ending cycle of car loans.

Then, we finally did something different. We paid off our vehicles. Suddenly, we had an extra $1,000 a month. That was money we had been throwing away for years. Money that wasn't building our future—just going straight into interest and car payments. That realization changed everything. Instead of spending that money on another car loan, we put it to work. We built up our emergency fund. We started investing. And for the first time, we truly understood what it meant to make our money serve a purpose.

That's what financial literacy does—it empowers you to make better choices. It helps you break cycles that aren't serving you and replace them with habits that build wealth, security, and peace of mind.

If there's one piece of advice I wish everyone knew—and actually applied—it's this: **Give every single dollar you earn a job.**

When you assign a purpose to every dollar, you control your money rather than let it control you. It stops you from overspending, living above your means, and making financial choices that set you back. Warren Buffett said it best: *"Do not save what is left after spending. Instead, spend what is left after saving."*

That's the mindset shift that changes everything. The difference between struggling and thriving isn't how much money you make—it's how well you manage what you have. And that's exactly why this book exists: to give you the knowledge you need to become a master of your money.

KEY TAKEAWAYS

- Financial literacy is essential for creating stability, avoiding costly mistakes, and positioning yourself to take advantage of financial opportunities. Without it, you risk falling into debt, missing out on investments, and struggling with financial insecurity.

- No matter your income level, financial literacy is crucial. High earners can still drown in debt if they spend beyond their means, while those with lower incomes can fall into predatory lending traps without the right knowledge.

- Waiting to start saving and investing is one of the biggest financial mistakes people make. The earlier you start, the more you benefit from compounding, and every year of delay significantly reduces your long-term wealth.

- Financial stress affects mental health, decision-making, and relationships. Poor money management leads to anxiety, strained marriages, and a cycle of bad choices—but taking control of your finances improves both your well-being and personal connections.

- A simple shift in perspective—like giving every dollar a job—can transform your financial future. When you prioritize saving over spending and make intentional choices with your money, you gain control, security, and long-term prosperity.

CHAPTER TWO

Assessing Where You Are
Financially and Taking the
First Step Forward

If you don't know where you are financially, how can you figure out where you're going? Before you start trying to improve your finances, you need a baseline—a real, honest look at where you stand. I always tell my clients they have to document everything related to their money- income and expenses. That means writing down your income, listing out all of your expenses, and getting clear on exactly what's coming in and going out. When you see those numbers in black and white, it's a reality check. If you're spending money without knowing how much you have to spend, and at the same time, you have no idea how much you're spending or what you're spending it on; you're stuck in a cycle. A vicious cycle that keeps you from ever making progress. You're working hard, but at the end of the month, you're wondering, *Where did all my money go?*

Remember this: **What is not measured cannot be improved. If you don't track it, you won't change it.**

When I work with my clients, the very first thing we do is take a financial snapshot. Before talking about fixing credit, building savings, or investing, we stop and get a complete picture of their current situation.

Here's what that looks like:

- We break down income—how much they bring in and from where.
- We document expenses—everything from rent or mortgage to that daily coffee stop.
- We discuss financial goals—what they ultimately want to achieve.

Once we lay that out, we have our starting point. This is what we will measure against moving forward. Every strategy and decision will be based on improving *this* picture. As we go, we can look back and see how far they've come.

Understanding Your Financial Picture

If you want to take control of your financial future, you need to look at how your income, expenses, debt, net worth, and savings all work together. Here's what you need to assess:

1. Income

Your income is the driving force behind everything else. It determines how much you can save, what assets you can buy, and how quickly you can pay off debt. Most of us rely on earned income from our jobs or businesses unless we've inherited wealth or received monetary gifts. But for the majority, income dictates the rest of our financial reality.

2. Expenses

Understanding where your money goes is as important as knowing how much you make. Break your expenses down into two categories:

- Fixed expenses (rent/mortgage, insurance, car payments)
- Variable expenses (groceries, dining out, entertainment)

Consistently tracking these will help you identify spending habits and adjust where necessary.

3. Savings & Emergency Fund

Do you have savings set aside? If an emergency happened today, could you cover it without going into debt? Your emergency fund should cover at least three to six months of expenses, and beyond that, you should be working toward long-term savings goals.

4. Debt

Your debt impacts everything from your credit score to your ability to save and invest. You need to be aware of:

- Your total debt balance
- The interest rates on your debt
- Minimum payments and payoff strategies

The goal is to make sure your debt isn't consuming your financial future. If you have a lot of consumer debt (credit cards/ loans, etc.) with high interest rates, it is important to pay these off as soon as possible.

5. Net Worth

Your net worth is a key financial indicator. It's your total assets minus your total liabilities. This number can be positive or negative; if it's negative, it's time to focus on reducing debt and building assets.

A common way to estimate where your net worth should be is by using this formula:

(Your annual income) x (your age) ÷ 10 = Target Net Worth

For example, if you're 35 and earning $65,000 a year, your target net worth would be $227,500.

This matters for retirement because your net worth needs to generate enough income to support you when you stop working. The best way to build wealth is by acquiring assets that appreciate over time—things like real estate, investments, or businesses that grow in value.

The more clearly you understand these numbers, the better decisions you'll make. Every financial move should improve your overall net worth, not just your short-term cash flow. It all starts with knowing where you stand today.

When to Reassess Your Financial Situation

At a minimum, you should reassess your finances once a quarter to ensure you progress toward your short-term and long-term goals. For some people, a monthly check-in might be necessary, especially if they're actively working on paying off debt, adjusting their budget, or dealing with financial uncertainty.

Certain life events or warning signs should prompt you to review your financial picture immediately. Here are some indicators to be aware of:

- You're struggling to cover expenses. If you consistently run out of money before payday or rely on credit cards to make ends meet, your spending and income need attention.
- A major life change occurs. Events like having a child, getting married, going through a divorce, changing jobs, or having an elderly parent move in with you all impact your financial plan.
- You experience job loss or a change in income. If you're unemployed, switching careers, or getting a raise, your budget and savings strategy need adjustments.
- You face a significant unexpected expense. If your emergency fund isn't enough to cover it, you may need to reassess how much you're setting aside for emergencies.
- You're making a lot of unnecessary purchases. If you notice that impulse buys or lifestyle creep are eating into your goals, it's time to reset and refocus.
- Your financial goals have changed. If you've set new short-term or long-term goals—like saving for a home, retiring early, or starting a business—you need to update your plan to reflect those changes.

Regular check-ins prevent small issues from turning into big problems. The goal is to stay in control, adjust as needed, and keep moving forward.

Common Mistakes When Assessing Finances

When people try to evaluate their finances, they often make the same mistakes that keep them from making real progress. One of the biggest issues I see is avoiding reality altogether. Many don't want to check their bank balance, look at their debt, or assess their spending habits because they fear what they'll find. But ignoring the problem won't make it disappear—it only worsens it. Facing your situation is the first step toward improving it.

Another major mistake is not having a plan. Too many people assume that they're fine as long as they're earning money. But without a roadmap or plan, you're just guessing. Whether saving, paying off debt, or investing, you need measurable goals to track progress. Saying, *"I want to save more money,"* isn't enough. You need to define how much and by when.

Then, there are cash flow issues—not knowing where your money is going. If you don't track your income and expenses, you might feel like you're constantly struggling to keep up. Often, people underestimate their expenses or overestimate how much they can afford. That leads to overspending on non-essentials, like impulse purchases, unused subscriptions, or small daily expenses that quietly add up.

Debt mismanagement is another common trap, especially with high-interest credit cards. Many people only make minimum payments, not realizing how much interest they rack up. Without a plan to prioritize and pay down debt efficiently, they end up paying far more than they should.

Not having an emergency fund is another misstep. Life happens; unexpected car repairs, medical bills, or job loss can throw everything off track. Without at least three to six months of living expenses saved, one emergency can spiral into financial hardship.

I find that some people also fail to check in on their investments. They put money into retirement accounts or stocks but never adjust their strategy as their life circumstances change. The same goes for insurance coverage. As life changes, your auto, home, life, or disability insurance should too.

Lastly, there's credit and tax planning. Many people don't monitor their credit reports for errors or fraud, which can impact their financial opportunities. When it comes to taxes, some wait until filing season instead of planning throughout the year, missing deductions and overpaying when they could be using that money during the year instead of getting a large one-time refund.

How to Stay on Track

Avoiding these mistakes comes down to being realistic and intentional with your money. That starts with what I call the B-word—yes, budgeting. If you don't like calling it a budget, think of it as a spending guide or money allocation plan, whatever helps you stay accountable. Giving every dollar a job is the key to financial security. You're setting yourself up for long-term success when you pair that with financial education, smart planning, and regular check-ins.

Small, Simple Actions to Improve Your Finances

Ever heard the saying, "How do you eat an elephant? One bite at a time." That's how you need to approach improving your financial situation. It might feel like a tall task at first, but taking small, manageable steps can completely transform your money matters.

To make it easy, I like to use **The ABCs of Financial Change**:

- **A** – Acknowledge your current financial state. Take an honest look at where you stand.

- **B** – Budgeting. (Yes, the B-word again!) Creating a plan for your money gives you control.
- **C** – Commit to your financial future. Make financial growth a priority.
- **D** – Don't waste money on unnecessary things. Cut back on non-essential spending.
- **E** – Educate yourself. The more you learn about finances, the more empowered you become.

This is just the beginning. For the complete A-Z list of small actions you can take, visit my website: **thewealthripple.com**.

Breaking Through Financial Fear

I'll never forget one of my clients—a grandmother who desperately wanted to improve her financial situation, not just for herself but also for her granddaughter. She knew she had been making poor decisions, but she was stuck in a cycle of avoidance, paralyzed by the fear of where to start and overwhelmed by how much needed to be done.

When we first sat down to talk, she was hesitant. Like so many people, she had convinced herself that looking at her finances would only confirm her worst fears. But as we started going through things together, something shifted.

We assessed her income, expenses, and credit profile and outlined achievable goals. I walked her through the basics of creating a budget that worked for her, beginning to pay off debt without feeling suffocated and setting aside money for emergencies without depriving herself of a life she could enjoy. Most importantly, we worked together and created a personalized roadmap that was tailored to her needs rather than generic advice.

At first, she was still nervous. But as the weeks went by, she transformed. She stopped dreading our check-ins and started looking forward to them. She began celebrating small wins, like seeing her debt shrink and watching her savings account grow. She automated her bill payments, was conscious about her spending, and built confidence in her financial decisions.

And then came the moment she had been working toward: she was finally on track to purchasing a home for her and her granddaughter. A goal that once felt impossible was now within reach because she had faced her finances head-on.

And so can you.

Start with a financial check-in. Write down your income, expenses, and debts. Be honest about where you are. Then, commit to change. Educate yourself. Budget with intention. Pay down your debt. Build your savings. Every small step you take today is shaping the financial life you'll have tomorrow. So take that first step. Your future self will thank you for it.

KEY TAKEAWAYS

- If you don't measure your finances, you can't improve them. Taking an honest financial snapshot of your income, expenses, debt, and savings is the first step to gaining control over your money.
- Your financial picture includes more than just income. Tracking fixed and variable expenses, building an emergency fund, managing debt, and understanding net worth are all essential to long-term success.
- Regular check-ins help you stay on track. Major life changes, unexpected expenses, or financial struggles are all signals to reassess your plan.
- Avoid common mistakes like ignoring your problems, lacking a clear financial plan, overspending, mismanaging debt, and failing to prepare for emergencies. Small, intentional adjustments can prevent bigger problems.
- Facing your finances can be intimidating, but change starts with tiny, consistent steps. Acknowledge your situation, budget wisely, commit to learning, and make smart money choices.

PART TWO

MASTERING THE ESSENTIALS OF FINANCIAL STABILITY

CHAPTER THREE

The Psychology of Money

It's time to examine your money mindset. I'm talking about your foundation: what you were taught or *not* taught about money growing up, what you saw your parents or caregivers doing with money, and how that shaped your own beliefs.

Think about you as a child. What did you see? What did you hear? Were your first memories about money tied to fear, shame, guilt, or excitement and confidence? All of that matters. Those early experiences are the roots of how you see and handle money today.

How you feel about money—whether it makes you anxious, hopeful, embarrassed, or motivated—connects back to your original exposure. Those early beliefs create your mindset, which influences everything: how you spend, save, invest (or don't), and plan for your future. Your emotions around money, your behaviors with money, and your financial decision-making stem from that internal story you've been telling yourself, maybe without even realizing it.

We need to take an honest look at your money psychology so you can identify what needs to change. Maybe there's something you need to adjust or a belief you need to completely let go of. Once you understand where those thoughts and habits come from, you can finally start making better financial decisions. These are decisions that actually get you excited about your future—not just financially but personally.

What You Saw Growing Up Matters

Most of us are doing exactly what we saw growing up when it comes to money. Whether we realize it or not, we model or emulate what we witnessed. How our parents or family members handled money left a deep impression on us.

If you grew up in a household where bills were paid on time, the lights stayed on, the fridge stayed full, and things were stable, then that planted a seed. That seed said, "Hey, when you earn money, pay your bills. Be responsible. Make sure you're living comfortably." That becomes your foundation. So, without even thinking about it, you might be the kind of person who always pays things early, avoids debt, and feels secure in your decisions surrounding money.

But on the flip side, maybe you experienced instability—maybe utilities were turned off, your family's car was repossessed, or there were nights without food. That kind of experience can create a *scarcity mindset*. And that can show up in two different ways.

You might either:

- Always feel like there's never enough money, no matter how much you have, or
- Be determined never to go back to that feeling again—so you manage every penny and focus on building an abundant life with intention.

Both of those responses come from the same place: the emotional experience of lack.

Let me give you a personal example. My dad was the main breadwinner in our family. He worked hard and earned the money, and my mom—who also worked —was the one who actually wrote the checks and paid the bills. I remember this one day clearly. I was a teenager, had just gotten my driver's license, and went downtown to pay their mortgage.

The mortgage at the time was just a little over $500. And to teenage me? That felt like a *lot* of money. I remember thinking, "Wow, this is what adulting really looks like." And let me tell you—now that I'm grown and paying my own mortgage? I'd *love* to have a $500 mortgage! But what stuck with me even more was how serious my dad was about paying bills on time. That was his thing. He was *and still is* a stickler about it!

I'll be honest—just because you see something as a kid doesn't mean you follow it immediately. When I got older, went off to college, and got a little freedom, I didn't always follow the example I saw. But the foundation was there, and eventually, I came back to it.

Your past experiences with money, good or bad, are shaping your money behavior today. That's why it's so important to understand them. Because when you know where your beliefs came from, you can start shifting them toward something better.

Limiting Money Beliefs

Your money mindset can significantly hold you back financially. If you constantly think, *"There's never enough,"*

"I'm always going to struggle," or *"I'm just not good with money,"* then that mindset is running the show—and not in a good way.

Some people avoid budgeting altogether. They don't plan or save because they're chasing that instant gratification: *"I worked hard—I deserve this right now."* But when you're living in the moment like that and not thinking long-term, it's easy to stay stuck in a cycle of financial stress.

And then there's the emotional baggage. Some people were taught growing up that *money is evil* or that *rich people are bad.* So now they feel ashamed to talk about money. They avoid it. They don't want to deal with it. And deep down, they believe they cannot manage it well.

Do you want to know if you have a limiting belief about money? Listen to how you talk about it. Do you say things like:

- "Money doesn't grow on trees."
- "I'll never get ahead."
- "I hate thinking about money."
- "Only greedy people care about money."

If those phrases sound familiar, you're not alone. But those thoughts are limiting beliefs. And they're keeping you from stepping into the financial life you deserve.

Scarcity vs. Abundance:
Two Totally Different Mindsets

If you are trapped in a scarcity mindset, make it your goal to shift to one of abundance! This is a fun topic for me to share with you because it's a game-changer once you see the difference between scarcity and abundance thinking.

Let me break it down.

1. Planning Ahead

- **Scarcity mindset:** You only think about the *now*. You want things right away, even if it messes up your future. It's all about instant gratification.
- **Abundance mindset:** You think long-term. You plan. You invest. You build toward something better.

2. Spending Money

- **Scarcity mindset:** You're anxious every time you spend. Even small purchases stress you out. Or, just the opposite, you overspend on retail therapy.
- **Abundance mindset:** You enjoy spending because you've planned for it. You know you're not hurting yourself financially by treating yourself.

3. Earning Money

- **Scarcity mindset:** You believe there are only a few good jobs out there. So even if you hate your job, you stay because it pays "good money." You think the only way to make more is to work harder.
- **Abundance mindset:** You believe there are *endless* ways to earn money. You take risks, explore opportunities, and understand that sometimes you have to spend money to make money.

4. Saving and Investing

- **Scarcity mindset:** You're afraid to invest. You think, *"I'll lose everything,"* so you hoard cash or don't do anything with your money.
- **Abundance mindset:** You see money as a tool. You let it *work* for you. I read somewhere that eventually, *80% of your income should come from your money making money—not from you working for it.* That's the goal.

5. Talking About Money

- **Scarcity mindset:** You don't talk about money. You're ashamed, or you think it's taboo.
- **Abundance mindset:** You're not afraid to talk about money. In fact, you *like* talking about it—sharing ideas,

learning about new opportunities, and helping others grow, too.

Take a moment and check yourself. Where do you see scarcity showing up in your life? And where can you begin shifting into abundance? That mindset shift is *everything* to building the financial future you want. It's not too late to change. The first step is admitting there's a problem. You have to acknowledge it. That's the beginning of any transformation. If you avoid talking about money or don't see money as a tool to help you but rather something taboo or stressful, then just saying, *"I need to change the way I think about money,"* is huge. That's your starting line.

Now, let's talk about what comes next...**rewiring your mindset.**

- **Educate Yourself**

  You've probably heard me say this a few times already in this book—and you're going to hear it again: *education is key*. Learning about how money works, understanding financial principles, and knowing your options can completely change your thoughts about money. The more you know, the more confident and in control you'll feel.

- **Practice Gratitude**

  Don't focus on what you *don't* have. Focus on what you *do* have. Make a list. When you start to recognize the things you *do* have—no matter how small—you'll begin to appreciate them more. That appreciation shifts your energy. It opens the door to abundance.

- **Stop Comparing Yourself to Others**
Please hear me on this: someone else having more than you does *not* mean you can't have more, too. There is enough money and opportunity to go around. Your journey is *your* journey. Stop measuring your progress against someone else's timeline.

- **Focus on Growth**
Ask yourself, "How can I improve?" "What can I do to put myself in a better situation?" That's where your focus should be—on your growth, on getting better, stronger, and more financially aware—step by step.

The Money Habits That Keep You Stuck

As well as mindset, some habits are just financially damaging. If you've been struggling, it might be because of one (or more) of these patterns.

Living Above Your Means

This is the biggest one. People are out here ordering steak on a burger budget. If you're spending more than you earn, you're digging a deeper hole. The goal isn't to deprive yourself, but you've got to live *below* your means, not above it.

Racking Up Bad Debt

Credit cards? They are *not* free money. That's a loan. And it comes back—with *interest*. I've seen credit card rates as high as 26%, 29%, even 32%. If you keep adding to that kind of debt, you're holding yourself back. That money could be going toward building your future, but instead, it's getting eaten up by interest payments. And chances are you are repaying this debt and wasting your money on things you don't even remember or no longer use.

Not Having a Plan

If you don't have a plan for your money, you're just letting it flow out with no direction. Every dollar needs a job. If you're spending without tracking, you'll never get ahead. You've got to plan for the future—not just live for today.

And don't fall for those buy-here, pay-here places or fast-cash spots. Sure, they'll hand you money quickly, but guess what? In a week or two, that money has to be paid *back*—and usually with extra fees and interest. That's how people end up even deeper in the hole.

Not Saving Anything

If you're spending everything you make, there's nothing left to protect you in an emergency. There's no foundation to build on. Saving—even just a little—is how you begin to take control.

Only Trading Time for Money

This one's a mindset shift. A lot of us think the only way to make money is to exchange our time for it. But that's not true. Remember what I said earlier—you want to get to a point where *your money is making money for you.* That's what investing is all about. That's what financial freedom is about.

Making Money Decisions with Logic, Not Fear

One of the biggest challenges I see is people making financial decisions out of fear or emotion instead of from a place of logic and clarity. When you've been living in survival mode, it's easy to react instead of plan. But if you want to move forward, you have to change how you think and act around money.

It starts with looking beyond the present moment. So many people are stuck living for today without giving any real thought to tomorrow. But tomorrow *will* come. And with it, bills, responsibilities, and goals that still need your attention. So, plan for what's next instead of just reacting to the now. That's how you begin to make decisions based on logic, not fear.

Creating a money plan is a great way to ground yourself. When you have financial goals—both short-term and long-term—you give your money direction. And one thing that helps tremendously is automation. So many tools are available today that allow you to set up automatic payments for your bills. When you automate, you reduce the chances of missing a due date, which keeps you from getting hit with late fees and added stress.

The same goes for savings and investments. You can set things up so that money is automatically moved into a savings account, an investment account, or a retirement fund. That way, you don't even have to think about it—it happens consistently.

Now, if you're trying to break out of bad money habits, there are a few exercises that can help you gain awareness and change your behavior. One powerful thing you can do is pause before every purchase and ask yourself, "Does this align with my current or long-term financial plan?" That one simple question can stop you in your tracks and get you thinking before spending.

Another eye-opener is tracking every cent you spend for a full week. Write everything down—coffee, snacks, gas, subscriptions. When you do that, it becomes crystal clear where your money is going, and you'll quickly see the areas where you might need to pull back or readjust.

Something I love recommending is creating a "money win" journal. Any time you make a smart money move—no matter how small—write it down. Maybe you called your internet provider and got your bill lowered by $10. That's a win. Perhaps you skipped that $8 coffee shop latte and made one at home instead. That's a win, too. These little decisions add up, and tracking them gives you something to celebrate and build momentum around. It helps you shift your identity to someone who makes *good* money choices.

I also want to remind you that so many resources are available today to help you grow financially. You can start investing with as little as five dollars through micro-investing platforms. You can open a high-yield savings account and start earning better interest. And yes, all of this can be automated to make your financial life easier and more consistent.

Lastly, and most importantly, be acutely aware of the way you talk to yourself about money. If you're constantly saying things like, "I'm bad with money," or "I'll never get ahead," then guess what? You're reinforcing that story. Flip the script. Start saying things like, "I'm learning how to make smart money decisions," or "Every day, I'm getting better at managing my finances." Speak life into your financial journey. What you believe, you'll begin to see reflected in your actions. And what you say you can do, you *can* do. But if you keep telling yourself you can't, you never will.

From Scarcity to Stability

Let me share a story that brings everything we've talked about in this chapter full circle.

When she was in college, my daughter had what many of us would recognize as a scarcity mindset. She lived on a tight college budget, always worried she didn't have enough, and constantly thought about lack. That mindset left her feeling stuck, uncertain, and limited in what she believed was possible for her future.

But fast-forward to today—she's now an engineer, making really good money, and her mindset has completely transformed. One of the ways she measures her stability isn't by her bank account balance but by something deeply emotional and symbolic for her—her pantry and refrigerator. For her, if both of those are full, it means she's doing well. It means she's providing. That's her personal gauge of success and security.

And she's not just focused on the now—she's actively planning for what comes next. She's started investing, not only for herself but for her children. She opened custodial accounts for them. She's laying a foundation that will help her kids grow up with an abundance mindset right from the start. Her turning point came when she realized how grateful she was for being in a place where she could provide more than enough for her family. That gratitude gave her a whole new perspective—and a whole new relationship with money.

Money is more than just numbers. It's tied to our self-worth, upbringing, relationships, and mindset. How we feel about money spills into many other areas of our lives. That's why working on developing a positive and abundant money mindset is so important. Not just for the sake of your bank account but for your peace of mind, sense of security, and overall well-being. Your relationship with money doesn't have to stay stuck in the past. You *can* change it. You *can* learn new habits. You *can* re-write your story. And when you do? You're not just improving your own life—you're paving the way for a brighter, more stable future for the people you love.

KEY TAKEAWAYS

- Your early experiences with money—what you saw, heard, and felt—shape how you handle finances today, whether you know it or not.
- Scarcity thinking keeps you trapped in survival mode while shifting to an abundance mindset helps you plan, invest, and grow with confidence.

- Limiting beliefs like "I'll never get ahead" or "I'm not good with money" need to be identified and replaced with empowering truths.
- Small changes—like tracking spending, celebrating "money wins," and using automation—can transform your financial habits and reduce stress.
- You can rewrite your money story at any time, and when you do, you're not just building financial freedom for yourself—you're setting a new standard for generations to come.

CHAPTER FOUR

Budgeting Without Fear

Having a plan or a mission for your money is the cornerstone of being financially responsible for your present situation and future financial well-being. Without a plan, there's no real way to get ahead financially or to secure a solid future. You can't do it without a budget. Spending money without a plan reduces the probability of saving and making investments.

On the flip side, when you have a budget and know where your money is going in advance, it can help reduce your anxiety and stress around money. Instead of feeling like you're just surviving, you start taking charge. With a budget, you can create goals that are personal to you. Whether it's paying off debt, building up your emergency fund, purchasing your first home, or preparing for retirement—whatever it is, that list can go on and on.

And when you budget, you can actually plot out target dates for those goals because you'll know exactly how much money you have to commit to each one. It also gives you the chance to see if you need to make any adjustments to stay on track. Plus, a budget helps protect you from making money choices that don't align with what you truly want for your future.

I know that for a lot of people, just hearing the word budget makes them feel anxious or even ashamed. It triggers strong emotions. They think budgeting means bare bones, harsh restrictions, and a boring life. They may envision eating Ramen Noodles and shopping at Goodwill. Of course, that's an exaggeration—but you get the point.

That's not what budgeting is about at all. Once people begin to get real financial education, they understand why a budget is so important. Their mindset shifts from feeling stuck in scarcity and limitations to seeing budgeting as a tool for making positive, productive, growth-focused decisions. And contrary to popular belief, a budget isn't there to chain you down. It does the opposite by empowering you to make the kind of life you actually want possible.

There was a gentelman who absolutely hated the thought of budgeting. Just the idea of it made him feel like it was too hard, too overwhelming, and honestly, just not obtainable. He couldn't even picture himself sticking to a budget, let alone benefiting from one.

But after a while, he realized that there was no way he was going to get ahead or change his financial situation without a plan. He made the decision to bet on himself. He chose to trust that he could do it—not just for himself but for his family's future. When he shifted his mindset and started focusing on the many benefits of budgeting instead of all the reasons he thought it wouldn't work, everything started to change.

After deciding to budget, he acknowledged that it wasn't as complicated as he thought. In fact, looking back, he realized he should have done it a long time ago. Now, he's on the other side of it. He's looking forward to reaping all the benefits of being responsible with his money, and he's proud of the better choices he's making every day.

That's the power of taking that first step. It doesn't have to be perfect. You just have to start.

What a Simple and Effective Budget Really Looks Like

You don't have to overcomplicate things to create an adequate budget. Simply divide your money into broad categories, breaking it up into your needs, wants, and financial goals. One popular example you might have heard of is the 50/30/20 rule. That's where you allocate:

- 50% of your income for your needs,
- 30% for your wants, and
- 20% for your financial goals.

This is not one-size-fits-all. You can absolutely adjust those percentages to fit your unique situation. For example, if you need to save more aggressively, you might increase your percentage toward your financial goals. Or, if you need to focus on paying down extra debt, adjust the needs category slightly. If you are laser-focused on paying down debt or building your savings, drastically reduce the "wants" allocation until you achieve your goal. Although you shouldn't totally eliminate your wants, you won't feel deprived. It's flexible. This kind of structure is very different from those complicated budgets that drill down into micro-classifications and make you feel like you need a degree in accounting to manage your money.

Once you get used to budgeting and are more comfortable with it, you can make your budget more detailed. You can add layers and specifics that help you move toward bigger goals. But initially, it's all about keeping it simple, doable, and focused on building good habits that will take you where you want to go.

Be Real with Yourself

Right out of the gate, the most important thing you need is a reality check. You have to look at what you're working with regarding your income and expenses. Split your expenses into two categories:

- Fixed expenses like your mortgage, car payments, or anything that stays the same monthly.
- Variable expenses like your electric bill, credit card bills, groceries, and gas that can change monthly.

You need to have a realistic view of your money by actually tracking your spending. Pull out your bank statements. Look at your card transactions. Write it all down. You can't fix what you're not willing to face. A basic budget with broad categories doesn't have to be complex, but it does have to be honest.

Prioritizing When Money Feels Tight

Everything feels urgent when money is tight. It can be incredibly overwhelming. Here's how to break it down and remove some of that anxiety. Some non-negotiables have to come first:

- You need a place to stay—a roof over your head.
- You need food to eat.
- You need basic clothing and essentials.

Once you have those basics covered, that foundation will ease some of your financial stress.

Next, set aside a small amount for an emergency fund. Even if it's just a little at first, it matters. I know it can feel impossible to save money when you're living paycheck to paycheck. Sadly, about 78% of people today are in that situation. But I promise you that saving is possible when you prioritize it.

Create the simple budget we discussed above so you know exactly what's coming in and going out. You need that clear picture in front of you. Look for ways to decrease your expenses a little at a time. Every slight cutback helps.

At the same time, look for ways to earn extra income. You could pick up a second job for a short time, start a side hustle (there are many legitimate ways to earn extra income online), or even sell things you no longer use. The goal is to create some breathing room, so you have extra money to put away. And you don't have to do it all at once. Aim for that first milestone: saving $1,000. Once you have that foundation, your next goal is to build up three to six months' living expenses in your emergency fund.

After that, I recommend setting up automatic payments for at least the minimum amounts on your bills. This way, you can avoid late fees and protect your credit.

When you put these pieces in place—housing, food, emergency savings, and automated bills—you're not just surviving anymore. You have a plan. And having a plan is one of the fastest ways to calm that constant sense of urgency and take control of your money.

Managing Debt with Slow and Steady Wins

Keep the end in mind when you're staring down a mountain of debt and feeling hopeless. Paying off or even just reducing your consumer debt will free up money that can be used for so many better things. Instead of going toward interest and minimum payments, your money can finally start working for you, helping you build wealth and create the life you really want.

The first step is deciding which debt payment method feels right for you. Some people choose the Snowball Method, where they pay off their smallest debts first and build momentum with quick wins. Others prefer the Avalanche Method, where they first attack the debts with the highest interest rates to save the most money in the long run. Both methods work. The important thing is choosing the one that will keep you motivated to stay consistent and keep your eye on the goal.

I always recommend automating your bill payments to ensure you never miss a due date, especially when working hard to climb out of debt. I also encourage people to use visual progress trackers (visit my website to get free progress trackers at **thewealthripple.com**) so you can physically see things getting better over time. It might seem small, but watching your progress grow can be a huge boost when overwhelmed.

And please, don't forget to celebrate the small wins. Every time you make an extra payment or cross a debt off your list, take a moment to acknowledge it. Celebrate it. Those little moments of victory add up and remind you that you are making progress, even if it feels slow at first. These wins solidify that you can meet your goals and crush your debt!

Your Financial Turning Point

When someone finally starts budgeting effectively, you can see the changes immediately. They become much more confident.

They're no longer ashamed to talk about money. It's not a topic they avoid anymore. Their anxiety around money starts to diminish. You can hear it in their voice and see how they carry themselves. You'll notice they have some breathing room for the first time in a long time. Because of that, their entire financial outlook becomes more positive, hopeful, and filled with possibility.

Even more importantly, their mindset shifts. Mindset is everything. When you have a positive, empowered mindset about your money, you make decisions that benefit you.

Budgeting doesn't bury you in restrictions or force you into boredom. It gives you a plan and, ultimately, freedom. One step at a time, one decision at a time, you can relieve the stress that money might have caused you in the past. You can feel proud of how you handle your finances. You can begin living with confidence, security, and peace of mind. And it all starts with the decision to believe you are capable and worth it.

KEY TAKEAWAYS

- Budgeting empowers you to take control of your money and build the life you want, one smart decision at a time, instead of feeling restricted.

- A simple, flexible budget that prioritizes your needs, wants, and financial goals can reduce stress, create clarity, and set you up for success.

- Looking honestly at your real income and expenses is the first step toward creating a plan that works.

- Building even a small emergency fund and managing debt with a clear, motivating strategy are key to creating financial breathing room.

- True financial relief comes from shifting your mindset—confidence grows, anxiety shrinks, and you finally start living with freedom and purpose.

CHAPTER
FIVE

Protecting Yourself from Financial Traps

It's one thing to earn money, but it's another thing entirely to manage it well, protect it, and eventually grow it. And that starts with avoiding the traps that can wipe out your progress in a heartbeat. I know this from experience. When I was newly married, I found myself in a money bind. I honestly can't remember what I needed the money for; I felt desperate. So I did what I thought was my only option at the time: I went to a payday loan place.

It was a Friday—a payday. I went with a friend, and the line was literally out the door. That should've told me something wasn't right there. I borrowed $300, but I was able to pay it back with my next paycheck. I got lucky.

But the whole experience resonated with me—that line of people, that feeling of desperation, that mindset of "I need this money no matter the cost." It was a wake-up call. I promised myself I'd never end up in that position again, and I haven't. That moment made me start getting serious about managing my money better.

What Financial Traps Really Look Like

When I think about financial traps, here's what comes to mind:

- **Not budgeting.** If you don't know where your money is going, it's already going to the wrong place.
- **Living beyond your means.** Spending more than you make is a fast track to stress and debt.
- **Using credit for emergencies.** This is a big one—credit cards aren't an emergency fund. They're a trap when used this way.
- **Not having savings.** No emergency fund means one unexpected expense can send your whole budget spiraling.

- **Living only for today.** If you're not planning ahead, you're planning to stay stuck.

And then we have payday loans and title loan places, which I consider some of the biggest traps of all. They're set up to look like help when you're in trouble, but they come with high interest, short repayment windows, and long-term consequences. And for people already struggling financially, they create a cycle that's hard to escape.

These options are dangerous because they keep you in survival mode. They keep you broke. They keep you stressed. Most of all, they keep you uneducated about how money really works. Every time you fall victim to a payday or title loan, you're moving further and further away from financial stability and even further from financial freedom.

Once you recognize these traps for what they are, you can start to avoid them. Once you start avoiding them, you can finally build a solid foundation. That's where we're headed next.

The Ugly Truth About Payday Loans and Predatory Lenders

Payday lenders and predatory loan companies make it look *so* simple to borrow money. They don't check your credit. They make the application process quick and smooth. And they pitch themselves like they're the answer to your cash emergency. But what they don't tell you, and what most people don't realize until it's way too late, is the true cost of borrowing that money.

It's all buried in the fine print. The real business model of these lenders is to trap you in a loop you can't get out of. They are banking on the fact that you'll *need* to return once you borrow because most people can't pay off that loan in full after the initial two weeks. So what happens? You extend it. You roll it over. You pay more fees. And the interest keeps stacking. You can end up paying an annual percentage rate (APR) that can hit *400%*. That's not a typo. Four. Hundred. Percent. People don't look at that when standing there desperate, needing quick cash.

But that desperation is precisely what these lenders are counting on.

They're not transparent. They don't sit down with you and explain what you're getting into. Twenty-one states have either banned or imposed specific restrictions on these types of lenders because their practices are deemed harmful and predatory.

When you're in a moment of panic or pressure, it's easy to believe this is your only option. But you have to pause, take a breath, and make a decision that serves your future instead of sabotaging it.

Spotting Red Flags Before It's Too Late

Let's discuss how to recognize the warning signs *before* you fall for a scam or debt trap.

First, if something feels a little too easy, like you don't need to meet any qualifications or go through any review process, that's your first red flag. These companies will approve almost anybody. No credit checks. No questions asked. And while that might seem like a blessing when you're in a financial pinch, it's actually a setup.

Here's another major red flag: interest rates over 36%**.** That's a clear signal that you're dealing with a predatory lender. Most legitimate lenders, especially traditional banks or credit unions, stay well below that number. If you see APRs climbing sky-high, you're not getting help; you're getting hustled.

Also, be cautious if the company isn't a traditional, reputable financial institution. A name you've never heard of, an office in a strip mall, or worse, no physical address at all? Proceed with extreme caution. It's not only the brick-and-mortar traps you need to watch out for anymore. Scammers are everywhere now—online, in your inbox, and even in your text messages. And they've gotten good at sounding legit.

One of the most obvious red flags? **If someone asks you to pay money upfront to get money.** That is not how lending works.

If someone says, "Just pay us $200, and you'll get $50,000," run the other way. They'll try to pressure you. They'll say this is a limited-time offer or that you must act now. That urgency is a tactic to get you to act without thinking it through.

Look out for confusing or hidden fees buried in the fine print. Be especially cautious if the company claims to be affiliated with a reputable bank or well-known institution. Scammers will use logos, branding, and language that make them look official.

If something feels off, *trust your instincts.* Take a step back and do your homework. You deserve clarity, respect, and options that move you forward.

A Wake-Up Call

I've seen people stuck in payday loan cycles repeatedly, and I want to share a story about a woman named Sally. Sally lived paycheck to paycheck. She didn't have any savings set aside, and she panicked when her car broke down, the vehicle she needed to get to work. She borrowed $500 from a payday lender with every intention of paying it back with her next check. But as life would have it, something else came up before payday. So she rolled over the loan, paid the fee, and promised herself she'd catch up next time.

Except the next time came, and it happened again. And again.

Each rollover came with another $125 fee. And just like that, her $500 emergency turned into a financial snowball that kept growing. What changed for her was that she hit a breaking point. She had a moment of clarity and realized that unless she made *drastic* changes, this cycle was going to keep repeating. So she buckled down. She created a budget, something she'd never done before, and got laser-focused on paying that loan off once and for all.

She contacted the lender and arranged a weekly payment plan. Little by little, she chipped away at it until the debt was finally gone. She made it a point never to get caught in that trap again. She committed to building an emergency fund. Even if it was just $25 out of every paycheck, she set it aside—*for herself.* So the next time life threw her a curveball, she wouldn't have to rely on anyone else.

There Are Safer Options

I know when you're in the middle of a monetary crisis, it feels like there's no way out. But there *are* safer alternatives to payday loans, even if it doesn't feel like it in the moment.

One of the biggest issues is that many people who turn to payday lenders are considered "unbanked." That means they don't have a relationship with a traditional bank or credit union. If that's you, I encourage you to change that because building that relationship opens up better doors.

A lot of credit unions offer their members something called **PALs—Payday Alternative Loans.** These are small-dollar loans with much more reasonable terms, lower interest rates, and actual repayment plans. Some banks and credit unions even call them Second Chance loans (please note: don't get these from payday loan places or other predatory lenders!) They're designed to give you a hand without pulling you under.

Other safer options might include:

- A **credit card cash advance** (yes, the rate can be high, but it's still usually far better than a payday loan)
- **Borrowing from friends or family** (I know that's not always easy, but if there's someone you trust, it can save you a lot of pain)
- **Nonprofits or charities** in your area (many offer financial help and don't expect you to pay it back)

Of course, the best safety net is the one you build yourself. Even starting small with your emergency fund—as Sally did—can change everything.

Take Back Control

If you're reading this and currently stuck in one of these traps, you've got to stop the bleeding. No more rollovers. No more extensions. No more "just one more time." Because every time you extend, you're digging the hole deeper.

Start by doing whatever you can to come up with extra money. Sell things you're not using. Cut out the coffees, the takeout, the subscriptions, the non-essentials. Get ruthless about your spending just for now. Focus only on what you *truly* need: a roof over your head, transportation to work, food, and making the minimum payments on your other debts.

It might feel like a lot at first, but I promise you—*the sooner you get out of the cycle, the sooner you'll feel peace again.* There is so much relief on the other side of this. And once you're out, the key is never to go back. Prioritize that emergency fund, even if it's just $5 or $10 per paycheck. Start where you are at. The habit matters more than the amount. That's how you take back control.

And at all costs, avoid the traps we've covered here. Walk away from anything or anyone who doesn't have your best interest in mind. Financial freedom is not just for the wealthy. It's for the wise.

KEY TAKEAWAYS

- Financial traps, such as payday loans, living beyond your means, and using credit for emergencies, keep you stuck in survival mode and far from financial freedom.
- Predatory lenders count on your desperation and use hidden fees, sky-high interest rates, and pressure tactics to trap you in a costly cycle.
- Recognizing red flags like no credit checks, high APRs, and upfront payments is your first line of defense against scams and predatory lending.
- Safer alternatives exist, like PALs from credit unions, trusted friends or nonprofits, and, most importantly, building your own emergency fund.
- If you're in a trap right now, stop the bleeding immediately, get serious about budgeting, and commit to never going back. Financial peace is possible when you take control.

CHAPTER
SIX

Credit Confidence

Your credit score is a reflection of your overall financial well-being. When you have a good credit score, it demonstrates to lenders and creditors that you are responsibly managing your credit, which makes you a lower risk to them. And when you're seen as less of a risk, doors start to open to better opportunities, better interest rates, and better access to the life you want.

I remember when I first started to see the benefits of having good credit in my own life. I got a platinum American Express card, and my daughters were floored. They were like, *"Mom, you've really made it! You got monies!"* And honestly? I kind of felt like I had. That card is metal with no preset limit, and it came with perks I didn't even know existed.

I had been traveling for years, flying here and there, but I never knew about those fancy airport lounges. Now I do, and they're phenomenal. Whenever my husband and I travel, we make sure to arrive at the airport early to enjoy the lounge. Free food, mimosas, and a pleasant atmosphere—it's a different experience. And it's one I never would've had access to without learning how to manage my credit.

That might seem like a small thing, but it's symbolic of something bigger. It's a reward for taking control of my finances. And it's a great accomplishment for someone like me, who didn't grow up knowing anything about things like credit scores or financial perks. This chapter is important because I want you to experience that same kind of breakthrough.

Why Credit Really Matters

Credit is powerful, but only when used the right way. When you manage it correctly, your credit can help you gain access to things you may not be able to afford all at once. It can serve as a stepping stone to homeownership, business opportunities, or even just better terms on the essentials you need in your daily life.

However, having bad credit can be costly. And I mean in ways people don't always think about. Yes, it means higher interest rates, but it can also mean higher car insurance premiums. And these days, some employers even check your credit before they offer you a job. Imagine being denied a good job, not because you're not qualified, but because your credit isn't where it needs to be. With bad credit, you might be declined for loans, credit cards, or mortgages, and that list keeps growing. Having poor credit can make life more expensive in ways that add up quickly.

Let me give you an example. Say you go to a place like Rent-A-Center to get a washer and dryer. It might sound like a good deal when they say you can rent it for $29.99 a week. But let's do the math. That adds up to about $119 a month. Over 24 months that comes out to nearly $2,900 for a washer and dryer, which actually costs $1,675.

That's a $1,200 difference—money you're spending just because you didn't have good credit or the cash saved up to buy it outright. Having bad credit is *expensive*. You end up paying more for the same things that someone else is getting for less. The extra money you are paying in this case could be used instead for paying off debt, building your emergency fund, or investing. In other words, getting ahead and not spinning in the same place or spiraling backward in your finances.

When you know how credit works and you take control of it, you stop being stuck. You stop overpaying. And you build a better financial future, one wise decision at a time.

Credit Score Myths

One of the biggest misunderstandings I see is when people think their credit score doesn't matter. They'll say, "Oh, I'm not buying a house anytime soon," or "I don't need a credit card." However, the truth is that your credit affects more of your life than you think.

Another common myth is that people think they'll always have bad credit if they have bad credit now. That it's permanent. It's not. Your credit score is something you can work on. It's not just one number stuck in stone forever. You can rebuild it. You can improve it. You just need to understand how.

Something else I want to bring up is the free credit score sites, such as Credit Karma or Credit Sesame. A lot of people rely on those, and while they can give you a general idea, they use what's called a VantageScore. That's different from what most lenders actually look at. Most banks, mortgage companies, and other creditors are using your FICO score, not the VantageScore.

And there's not just one credit score. There are three major credit bureaus—Equifax, Experian, and TransUnion—and you will have a separate FICO credit score from each of them. That's because not every creditor reports to all three bureaus. When checking your credit, ensure you review all three reports. Each one matters <u>due to different lenders using only one or two of the three bureaus' credit scores.</u>

How to Take Control and Rebuild Your Credit Yourself

You don't need to pay someone else to fix your credit. You can absolutely do this yourself, and I'll walk you through the steps.

First, you need to get a real, accurate assessment of your credit. That means pulling your credit report from each of the three major bureaus mentioned above—Equifax, Experian, and TransUnion. You can get your credit reports for free from <u>annualcreditreport.com</u>. In 2023, the limitation was changed from one report per year per credit bureau to the ability to request one report from each of the credit bureaus per week. You'll want to go over each one carefully. Look at every line. Check for anything outdated, inaccurate, or even fraudulent. And if you find something that's not right, you have the power to dispute it. You can send a dispute letter directly to the credit bureau, explaining what's wrong. By law, they have to respond to you within 30 days in writing. If an error is found, it must be removed from your credit report!

Now, if you notice an account that's behind or close to going into collections, reach out to that creditor right away. Talk to them. See if they're willing to work with you. You may be able to set up a payment plan that prevents the account from being reported as a collection, which can significantly impact your credit score.

If you already have something in collections, it's not too late. You can still contact them and negotiate. Ask if they'll accept a reduced payment to consider the debt paid in full and get it in writing. You can also request that they delete the account from your credit report once it's paid. Some will agree to do that.

These are just a few simple things you can do on your own starting today. You don't need a middleman. You need the information, the willingness to act, and a little persistence. Not only can this improve your credit score, but it can also save you a lot of money in the long run.

The Truth About Credit Repair Companies

Credit repair companies are everywhere, and they always seem to be promising quick fixes. You've probably seen those ads that say, *"We'll raise your credit score 100 points in 30 days!"* But that's a major red flag.

First of all, there's no one-size-fits-all solution when it comes to credit repair. Every credit report is different. Every financial situation is different. So when someone guarantees they can raise your score by a certain number of points in a certain number of days? No one can predict that—not even the credit bureaus themselves.

Here's something else you should know: you should never pay someone upfront before they've done any work. If someone is asking you to prepay for credit repair services, that's another red flag. By law, they are not supposed to charge you until they've provided the service.

There are also additional warning signs. If a company tells you not to pay your bills or if they promise to remove accurate information like a bankruptcy or a legitimate collection account—that's not just bad advice. It's illegal. If something is accurate, it belongs on your credit report, even if it's not flattering. No company can legally make that disappear.

And if they ever tell you *not* to contact the credit bureaus yourself? That's a big one. You have every right to contact the credit bureaus directly. In fact, I encourage you to do just that. It's your credit, your money, and your future—don't let anyone convince you that you have to go through them to fix it.

So before you hand over any money, do your homework. Understand your rights. And most importantly, know that you already have the power to improve your credit without paying someone else to do what you can do for yourself.

My Personal Credit Wake-Up Call

I haven't always had great credit. When I was a young mom, I struggled. I had a credit card, and, like many people, I didn't fully understand how it worked. Nobody ever taught me. I didn't know that you weren't supposed to max out your card— even if it was within the credit limit they gave you. So I did just that. I maxed it out. And then, I found myself struggling to make the minimum payments.

I'll never forget one day I was out shopping for my daughters, and I pulled out my credit card to pay. The cashier ran it... and it was declined. I was mortified. I wanted to shrink right into the floor. That moment was such an eye-opener for me. I realized then that credit is not free money, no matter how it might feel when you're swiping that card.

One of the most important lessons I learned from that experience is that payment history matters *a lot*. Your payment history makes up 35% of your total credit score. So, after that moment of embarrassment, I made a decision. I committed to paying off that card. And I didn't use it again until I was financially ready—until I knew I could handle the payments and make them on time, every time. That turning point taught me about discipline, timing, and the importance of educating yourself before using financial tools. Because when you know better, you do better.

Everyday Habits That Keep Your Credit Score Strong

Once you've put in the work to build or rebuild your credit, the goal is to keep it strong, and some key habits can help you do just that.

Pay your bills on time. I can't stress this enough. And if you're able to pay them early? Even better. Remember, your payment history makes up 35% of your credit score. That's the single most significant piece. Missing even one payment can cause considerable damage.

To ensure you don't miss a payment, I recommend setting up auto-pay (which is the best option) or setting reminders. If you are able to make your payment before the due date, it is a good practice to do so before the statement closing date. This will result in a lower balance reported to the credit bureaus, which could improve your credit score.

The next biggest factor is **credit utilization**—that's the amount of credit you use compared to your total credit limit. And I'll be honest, I didn't know this when I was younger. I thought as long as I stayed under my limit, I was good. But that's not how it works. It's recommended that you keep your usage under 30% of your total credit limit. Using less shows that you're responsible and can manage your credit wisely. Paying off the balance each month ensures your utilization is favorable.

Together, those two factors—on-time payments and low utilization—make up 65% of your score. That's 357.5 out of the 550 possible points in your FICO score calculation. So, if you get those two right, you're already well on your way to maintaining a solid credit profile.

Now, let's talk about the rest of your credit score and how to avoid slipping backward after all your progress.

Length of credit history makes up 15% of your score. That's why it's so important *not* to close old credit cards, even if you've paid them off. I know it's tempting. You might think, "Well, I'm done with that one; I don't want to mess things up again." But unless you truly feel you'd fall back into bad habits, it's better to keep those accounts open. The credit bureaus calculate the average length of your credit across all accounts, so those older ones help boost your score.

That's why I recommend that parents add their kids as authorized users on a credit card they pay on time. It gives their children a head start by building a long history early. That time adds up, and it can make a big difference later in life when they want to buy a car, a house, or even apply for a job.

New credit is 10% of your score. That means applying for too many new cards or loans in a short amount of time can make you look like you're in financial trouble even if you're not. Lenders might assume you're desperate for credit or not managing your current accounts well. Be cautious about opening new lines of credit unless there is a genuine need.

And finally, **credit mix**—also 10%—is also important. It's beneficial to have a variety of credit types, like revolving accounts (credit cards) and installment loans (like car loans or mortgages). This indicates to lenders that you can manage various types of debt responsibly.

To sum it up, pay on time, keep your balances low, avoid closing your oldest accounts, be cautious when opening new ones, and maintain a healthy mix. These everyday habits really do add up.

It's Never Too Late to Turn Things Around

I had a client who knew he needed to fix his credit. He was motivated, but like most people, he didn't know where to begin. We sat down together, reviewed all three of his credit reports, and I created a personalized plan for him. We focused on two key areas: quick wins—the "low-hanging fruit"—and longer-term strategies that would require more time but still yield significant benefits.

His TransUnion score at the time was 681, and within two months, it had jumped to 709. That might not sound like a lot to some people, but it was everything to him because his goal was to get above 700. He did it.

The biggest shift for him was in his mindset. He went from believing he couldn't fix it to seeing, with real proof, that he could. Once he realized that consistent, focused action could move the needle, it changed everything for him.

Now, I always give a little disclaimer here—there's no guarantee that your score will increase by a certain number of points or that it'll happen within a specific timeframe. Everyone's situation is different. But what I can say is this: if you stay committed, stay informed, and follow through, you *will* see progress. And that's what credit confidence is all about.

If you've made mistakes in the past—missed payments, collections, or even bankruptcy —please know that where you are is not the end. You can always, always, always improve your credit score, no matter what has happened before.

Yes, certain events, such as bankruptcy, will remain on your credit report for several years. But that doesn't mean your future is ruined. With time, patience, and a genuine commitment to changing any bad financial habits, you *can* rebuild.

There are also steps you can take right now to make a difference. One of the fastest ways to see an impact on your credit score is to reduce the amount of money you owe, especially on credit cards that are close to their limit. Lowering your credit utilization can give your score a boost without waiting years for negative items to fall off.

And for those things you *do* have to wait out? That's okay—because, in the meantime, you can strengthen the other parts of your credit profile. You can make every payment on time, keep your balances low, avoid unnecessary new accounts, and show that you've learned from the past.

Helpful tools are available, such as secured credit cards, which are a great way to start rebuilding if you've been turned down for traditional cards. These accounts report to the credit bureaus just like regular cards do, and they help you show lenders that you're serious about managing credit responsibly.

Credit is more about being consistent than being perfect. Whether you're just starting out, digging yourself out of a tough spot, or simply trying to maintain the progress you've already made, you have the power to shape your financial story. No matter what that score says today, it can—and will—change with time, effort, and the right knowledge.

KEY TAKEAWAYS

- Your credit score isn't . It can be rebuilt with consistent effort, informed decisions, and time, regardless of your financial past.
- Paying bills on time and keeping credit card balances low are two of the most powerful habits for maintaining a strong credit score.
- Don't fall for credit repair scams—you can dispute errors, negotiate collections, and rebuild your credit yourself without paying someone else.
- Understanding how credit works, including common myths, score breakdowns, and the role of different credit bureaus, empowers you to take control.
- Credit confidence comes from small, smart moves repeated over time, and it's never too late to start making them.

PART THREE
GROWING YOUR WEALTH AND LEAVING A LEGACY

CHAPTER
SEVEN

Investing Made Simple

We've already walked through some major financial funda-mentals—budgeting, understanding what's coming in and what's going out, and paying down debt. All of those steps have been leading you to this point. Once you've got a handle on your money, you're finally in a position to begin investing.

I learned firsthand, just by watching people in my own family, the massive difference that smart investing can make. Those who invest wisely have peace of mind and security. They're not stressing about what happens next. But for those who didn't invest, there's a lot more financial insecurity, and that uncertainty becomes more painful the older you get.

You might be thinking, *"That sounds great, Cassandra, but I don't have any extra money to invest."*

Investing is not optional. It's mandatory if you want a future that feels different from your present. If you're telling yourself you don't have enough to invest now, then I promise you, you will not magically have enough later unless something changes.

The good news is **you don't need a lot to get started.** I'll break that down for you as we go, but I want you to remember this upfront—it doesn't matter how much cash you have right now. Just get started and let time and consistency work in your favor.

The $5 a Week Strategy

Let me share a real story from my own family because this is the kind of thing that shows you just how possible investing can be, even if you start small.

My daughter started using one of those micro-investing apps, specifically **Stash.** She began by putting in just $5 a week. That's it. Five dollars. You can't even buy a combo meal for that anymore, but she used it to purchase partial shares of stock. She also opened custodial accounts for her children.

Fast forward a few years, and the total balance across all of those small, consistent investments? Over **$15,000**. From five-dollar deposits.

She turned me on to Stash, and now I do the same. I make weekly contributions for each of my grandchildren. And instead of buying toys or clothes for birthdays and Christmas, I deposit $100 into their investment accounts. That money is a head start on their financial future. I honestly think it's one of the wisest choices I could make as a grandparent. These kids will grow up already ahead of the game because someone thought to plant the seeds early.

Another Easy Way to Begin—Even on a Budget

A second app I personally use is **Acorns**. It's just like Stash in the sense that you can get started with as little as $5. It rounds up your spare change from everyday purchases and puts it into investments for you. It's automatic. Simple. And it works.

So don't let the word "investing" scare you off. You don't have to have thousands, or even hundreds, to begin. Just five dollars and a willingness to be consistent can completely change your long-term picture.

The Eighth Wonder of the World:
Compound Interest

If there's one concept I want you to understand by the time you finish this chapter, it's compound interest. It's often called the "eighth wonder of the world," and for good reason. That phrase comes from Albert Einstein himself. He said:

> *"Compound interest is the eighth wonder*
> *of the world. He who understands*
> *it, earns it. He who doesn't, pays it."*

Compound interest is like magic. It's when your money starts earning interest, and then that interest earns interest, and then that interest earns even more interest, and so on. All you have to do is get the ball rolling and give it time to take effect. Time is the most important ingredient in this equation. The longer your money sits in an investment earning compound interest, the more it grows.

Here is a basic example so you can see how powerful this is:

Let's say you invest **$500 just once**. You don't add anything else. If that money earns an **8% annual return** and you leave it alone for **30 years**, guess how much you'd have?

About **$5,467**.

That's almost **$5,000 in interest**—just from sitting there, compounding year after year.

Now, take that same $500, still at an 8% return, but only leave it for **five years**. You end up with just **$744**. That's only **$244 in interest**. Same money, same rate, but way less time.

If you're curious and want to play around with your own numbers, there's a free tool I love called The Calculator Site at <u>www.thecalculatorsite.com</u>. You can plug in how much you want to invest, how often, and for how long, and it'll show you just how much that money can grow over time.

Should You Wait to Invest Until You're Out of Debt?

I get this question all the time: *"Should I wait to invest until I've paid off all my debt?"*

No. Start now.

Even if you're still paying down debt, and honestly, most people are, you should still invest whatever you can. It doesn't have to be a lot. It just has to be something. I'm not saying ignore your debt. It's just the opposite. Take a good, honest look at your budget. Be intentional. Make adjustments wherever you need to so that you can do both—pay off debt and invest at the same time, even in small amounts.

If you're not sure how to tackle your debt, try one of the proven strategies out there. Use the **snowball method** (where you pay off your smallest debts first for quick wins) or the **avalanche method** (where you pay off the highest-interest debts first to save more over time). Select the one that best aligns with your mindset and financial habits. Continue to increase your investment as your debt decreases.

If You're Afraid to Invest, You're Not Alone—But Don't Let That Stop You

Many people are scared to invest. Maybe that's you. Perhaps you're thinking, *"What if I lose my money?"* or *"This sounds way too complicated for me."*

Most of that fear comes from not having the knowledge *yet*. It's not that you're incapable; it's just that you haven't been taught. And that's not your fault.

There are numerous ways to invest. Some are riskier than others, but that's the beauty of it—you get to choose what you're comfortable with. Once you educate yourself and do a little research, you can find low-risk investment options that match your comfort level and still give your money a chance to grow.

You cannot save your way into wealth. Yes, saving is essential. But saving isn't enough. You have to invest your money so that it can work for you, rather than you always working for it. That's how you create freedom.

Start with What Feels Easy and Build from There

If the thought of Wall Street makes your eyes glaze over or your stomach twists in knots, you don't have to be fluent in finance to start investing. There are beginner-friendly tools out there—apps like **Acorns, Stash, M1 Finance,** and **Ally**. These are what I consider *low-entry investment tools*. You don't need a financial advisor to walk you through a hundred different stocks or mutual funds. All it takes is $5 and opening an account right from your phone.

These apps are designed to be user-friendly, with simple language and straightforward steps. You can choose what kind of things you want to invest in, whether that's ETFs, mutual funds, or specific industries you care about. And you get to decide how often you wish to contribute: weekly, monthly, or even once a year. It's all up to you. These options are built for real people, not stock market pros, so there's no excuse to put it off.

Remember that the best day to start investing was yesterday. The second-best day is today.

You don't have to wait until everything is perfect. You don't need thousands of dollars or a degree in finance. Even if you are still paying off debt or have never invested before, the most powerful thing you can do is start small today. In five, ten, or thirty years down the road, you will look back and be so glad you did.

KEY TAKEAWAYS

- Investing isn't optional if you want to build long-term financial security. Starting small and starting now matters more than having a lot.
- Tools like Stash and Acorns make investing accessible with as little as $5, and consistency over time leads to powerful growth.
- Compound interest is your best friend. Time is the secret ingredient that multiplies even small investments into significant gains.
- You don't have to wait until your debt is gone to invest; it's possible—and smart—to do both at the same time with a solid plan.
- Fear and lack of knowledge are normal, but they don't have to hold you back. Start with what feels easy, learn as you go, and let your money work for you.

CHAPTER EIGHT

Inspiring Change in Your Family and Community

All of the efforts you have put into accumulating wealth by budgeting, paying off debt, and maybe even investing shouldn't stop with you. It shouldn't just benefit your immediate household. The bigger picture, the real legacy, is how you use that knowledge and progress to impact your family for generations to come and even help the community around you.

I've seen what happens when that doesn't take place. Personally, I've watched people pass away without a plan. No assets left behind, no structure in place—just debt. And instead of receiving an inheritance, the loved ones they left behind inherited financial hardship. Dr. Boyce Watkins said "Generational wealth is the throne your children should inherit, not your debt." The work you're doing right now can and should spare your family from that burden.

You've worked too hard to build wealth for it to be lost or misdirected after you're gone. Estate planning ensures your assets go to the right people and the right causes. It gives *you* the power to decide where your money and property go, rather than leaving it to the courts and the government. Whether it's your spouse, your kids, your grandkids, or a charity you care about, your estate plan puts your wishes in writing and honors them.

Without it, everything you've worked so hard for could end up in probate court. The state will step in and decide who gets what—and trust me; they're not going to make those decisions based on love or loyalty. On top of that, your estate could be hit with taxes that eat away at the value you've created.

Estate planning isn't just for the wealthy. It's something *responsible* people do.

Start the Conversation—Even If You're Just Learning Too

You don't need to be a financial expert to educate the people you love. Even if you're just figuring this stuff out yourself, you can bring others along with you. Start simple. Discuss money with your children or young adults. Teach them the basics of budgeting and how to distinguish between a want and a need. These conversations don't have to be perfect. Just make them part of your everyday life.

Invite your kids to join you in any financial education workshops you're attending. Let them read the books that are helping you. Share the videos, the podcasts, or whatever you're learning from. And most importantly, be the example. Show them what it looks like to manage money with intention. That's the lesson they'll never forget.

Passing down money without financial knowledge is like handing someone a car without teaching them how to drive. They might get lucky for a little while, but chances are, it's not going to end well. It's essential—mandatory even—that future generations are taught how to manage, grow, and protect money. I can't stress that enough. Having money is great. But if you don't have the skills or the mindset to handle it, that money's going to disappear fast.

There's a statistic I came across that stuck with me: after three generations, more than 90% of a family's wealth is gone. Think about that. Three generations. And the reason is simple—no one taught the next generation how to keep it going. Or the next generation didn't heed the wisdom of those who came before them. Either way, the result is the same: the money's gone.

Teach Them There's More Than One Way to Earn

Another thing that is so important to pass on is the power of entrepreneurship. Many people grow up thinking that the only way to earn money is to get a job and work for someone else. And sure, there's nothing wrong with having a job. But I believe it's just as important to teach your kids that they can make money on their own terms. That they can start a business. That they can create something valuable and be paid well for it.

That kind of thinking opens up doors, gives options, and plants the seed early so that they don't have to stay stuck or settle. They can create the life they want—financially and other-wise—by learning how money works and using that knowledge to their advantage.

Building Wealth Starts With Your Mindset

If you're starting from scratch or trying to recover from financial hardship, you can still absolutely create generational wealth. But it's got to start in your mind. That shift is the first step. You must let go of the shame and guilt associated with past mistakes. You're not your past, and you're not stuck. Abundance is possible. Start believing you deserve financial peace.

Once your mindset is in the right place, then it's time to take action. Learn how to build and protect wealth. Make wise money decisions. And don't wait for "the right time" to begin investing—do it as early as you can. Warren Buffet said, "The best time to invest was yesterday; the next best time is now." The earlier you start, the more time your money has to grow through compound interest.

Also, don't just put all your eggs in one basket. Diversify your portfolio to minimize reliance on a single type of investment. And please—don't depend on a single paycheck. One of the most significant ways to grow your wealth over time is by creating multiple streams of income. Your 9-to-5 can be your base, but it shouldn't be your only source.

Your Transformation Can Inspire Those Around You

When you get your finances in order, it naturally starts to ripple out and affect everyone around you, including your family, church, workplace, and neighborhood.

Some of my family members, including my brother, are a great example. Every single year, they sponsor and volunteer to put on this fabulous Fourth of July fireworks show for the kids and families in the community where we grew up. They don't do it for praise—they do it because they can. It brings immense joy to everyone who attends.

I also have a mentor who's financially secure and never hesitates to make large donations to her church. Giving back is now an integral part of her lifestyle. A former boss of mine had planned well and built wealth with her husband, so she was in a position to donate her *entire* salary to nonprofit organizations she was passionate about. Imagine that—being able to give your whole paycheck away because your financial foundation is that solid.

Becoming the Role Model Your Family Needs

I once worked with someone who became a true financial role model for her entire family. When we first met, she didn't have much financial education. Like so many people, she hadn't been taught the basics. But once she started learning, she took it seriously. She made better decisions, she got strategic, and it paid off.

She was eventually able to qualify for a home loan and buy her very first house. She was the *first person in her family* ever to become a homeowner. That changed everything. That one move shifted her family's trajectory. She broke the cycle, and because of her, other family members started asking questions, learning more, and making smarter financial decisions with their money, too.

Stop Treating Money Like a Taboo Topic

One of the biggest things holding families back from building generational wealth isn't money itself—it's the way we talk (or *don't* talk) about it. In many families, money is treated as a taboo subject. No one wants to talk about it openly, and sometimes, that silence is rooted in shame. Maybe someone feels embarrassed about their financial mistakes. Perhaps they wish they'd taken better opportunities but didn't. Maybe they just don't know what to say because they never learned how money works themselves. But avoiding the conversation doesn't help anybody. It just passes the same silence—and the same struggle—on to the next generation.

And then there's this myth that if your parents or grandparents struggled financially, then your family is just destined to struggle forever. That is absolutely not true. One person—*you*—can decide to break that cycle and lead your family in a completely different direction. Financial struggle is not your legacy unless you let it be.

If you want to create wealth and pass it on, your family needs to become comfortable discussing money—out loud, together, and often. There are so many tools that can help. You've got budgeting apps. You've got spreadsheets. You can start by tracking your money together—what's coming in, what's going out—and make decisions as a family.

Let your kids help when you're creating the family budget. Teach them the value of a dollar. Open custodial investment accounts for them and explain the process in a way they can understand. Bring them into family financial discussions as early as possible, and always share real-life examples that are age-appropriate and relevant.

Here's something fun you can do: create financial goals or milestones as a family. Task everyone—young and old—with coming up with creative ways to save or grow money. Have "no spend" days and think of ways to use what you already have. Maybe instead of going to the movies, plan a movie night in the backyard, or, instead of buying out for dinner, have a night when everyone cooks a meal together. Maybe the goal is a family vacation. Perhaps it's saving for a big purchase. Whatever it is, make it a team effort. There are many fun saving trackers available, or you can create your own and color them in as you save the dollar amount for each unit. You can celebrate after you have completed the entire sheet!

And while you're out and about, use everyday moments to reinforce the lessons. Like when you're at the store, and the kids are used to picking up five or six snacks—now they can learn to pick just two. Help them to pause and think about what they really need versus what they want at the moment. Or let them earn their own money. Help them set up a lemonade stand or run a simple business. They'll get a real-life taste of what it means to make, manage, and value money.

The more you do this, the more normal these conversations become. And that's the goal: to make discussions about money the *norm* in your home—not the exception, and definitely not something off-limits.

Pass It On—with Purpose and Passion

Once you've done the work to generate wealth in your family and you've laid the foundation to ensure that future generations are set up—you're in a position to create an even bigger impact.

And for many people who reach that level, it becomes natural to want to give back.

Because when you give your time, your resources, or your financial support, you help transform lives. You help transform communities. Your generosity can be the spark that changes someone else's entire future. So yes, take care of your family. Ensure that your children and grandchildren have the tools, knowledge, and mindset to manage what you've built. But don't stop there. Look outside your circle. Find those organizations, causes, or people you care deeply about and pour into them, too.

When you pass down your wealth, make sure you also pass down the *story* behind it. Tell your family what you learned, what you sacrificed, and what you wish you'd known sooner. Share the *financial finesse* it took to grow that wealth so they not only keep it going—they take it even further.

That's how real legacies are built. That's how generations are changed. And it all starts with you.

KEY TAKEAWAYS

- Estate planning is not just for the wealthy but for anyone who wants to protect their legacy and spare loved ones from future hardship.

- Start normalizing conversations about money within your family, even if you're still learning; being the example is the most powerful teaching tool.
- Building wealth begins with mindset. Let go of guilt and scarcity thinking, and make intentional financial decisions that support long-term growth.
- Teach the next generation how to earn, save, and invest through entrepreneurship and multiple income streams.
- Your financial transformation can spark change in your family and community, so pass it on with purpose, passion, and the story behind how you built it.

EPILOGUE

"You don't have to be perfect with money.
You just have to be purposeful."
– Stephanie O'Connell

First, I want to celebrate *you*. You made it through this book, and more importantly, you made a commitment to yourself. You chose to invest your time in learning how to improve your current and future financial well-being. It's not just your future self that will thank you—your future generations will feel the ripple effect of what you're doing right now.

When you started this journey, maybe you were struggling financially. Perhaps you just needed to improve your money management skills. Now that you have the mindset, the tools, and the knowledge, you can shift the trajectory of your finances in a more positive and profitable direction.

But if you don't do anything with what you've learned, the cost can be steep. Staying in the same place means continuing to spiral in the wrong direction, living paycheck to paycheck, feeling constant stress, and making decisions that hurt more than help. And let's not forget one of the biggest things that could cost you—time. The earlier you start investing, the more powerful that compounding interest becomes. Don't wait. Waiting is expensive.

Here are your next steps:

1. Decide and commit to at least *two* action items from this book.
2. Book your complimentary 30-minute consultation with me to discuss the next steps on your "Wealth Ripple" journey.
3. Visit **thewealthripple.com** to get access to more wisdom, tools, tips, and resources.

As you continue to move forward, your confidence will grow, your mindset will shift, and your future will look brighter than ever. You'll be a role model for your kids, a source of wisdom for your family, and someone your community can look to for guidance. The change starts with you.

Ready to take the next step in fulfilling
your desire to achieve wealth?

Book your life-changing *"Wealth
Ripple Action Call"* now.
This complimentary one-on-one call
is designed to help you apply what you
learned in this book and start the journey
of customizing your wealth action plan.

Change the financial trajectory of your
life and your future generations.

VISIT: thewealthripple.com

ABOUT
CASSANDRA M. THOMAS

Cassandra M. Thomas is a dedicated financial educator with a deep passion for helping individuals and families take control of their money and create a path toward lasting wealth. Witnessing how certain communities are systematically targeted to stay trapped in financial struggle fuels her relentless drive to reach them, with a powerful message: "This is not their destiny."

With years of experience guiding clients through financial challenges, Cassandra empowers people to assess their current situation, overcome financial setbacks, and make informed, confident decisions that lead to real progress.

She believes that financial freedom isn't just for the wealthy—it starts with small, intentional steps made consistently. Cassandra has taught both adults and school-age children the fundamentals of budgeting, credit, and saving, and is a strong advocate for making financial literacy accessible to every household.

Her credentials reflect her commitment to excellence and impact. She is a Board Certified Credit Consultant, Certified Credit Score Consultant, and Certified Credit Score Specialist. Additionally, through the National Financial Educators Council (NFEC), she is a Certified Financial Literacy Professional (CFLP) and a proud member of the United for Financial Literacy Advocacy Committee.